THE VALUE OF NAMES

BY JEFFREY SWEET

Revised Edition

DRAMATISTS
PLAY SERVICE
INC.

DEVELOPMENT AND PRODUCTION HISTORY

The Value of Names has evolved through several drafts into the form in which it appears here.

Commissioned by Actors Theatre of Louisville, the first version was developed with the invaluable assistance of members of the New York Writers Bloc. Comments in the wake of a reading at Ensemble Studio Theatre's 1982 Summer Conference also proved to be of great help. At this point, I would like to acknowledge my debts to Kate Draper, Conrad Bromberg, John Randolph, Sarah Cunningham, Donald Margulies and other members of the two organizations named above. I would also like to thank Jon Jory, the artistic director of Actors Theatre of Louisville, and Louisville's then literary manager, Julie Beckett Crutcher, for concise and supportive criticism during the development of the script. Thanks, too, to Corinne Jacker for her much appreciated support during the period when I was writing this.

The Value of Names received its first public performance on November 4, 1982 as part of Actors Theatre of Louisville's Shorts Festival. Emily Mann directed the cast, which included Larry Block as Benny, Robin Groves as Norma, and Frederic Major as Leo. A slightly expanded version of the script was used when it was revived on March 26, 1983 as part of Louisville's Humana Festival.

The second Louisville version of the script was also presented at Chicago's Victory Gardens Theatre, beginning March 30, 1983. The cast featured Shelley Berman as Benny, Jill Holden as Norma, and Byrne Piven as Leo. It was presented on a bill with the premiere of a companion piece called *George's File,* which featured Caitlin Hart as June. The production was directed by Sandy Shinner, who was also that theatre's literary manager. The very supportive and patient artistic director was Dennis Zacek. This production was subsequently transferred for an extended run at the Apollo Theatre Center in Chicago.

A slightly revised version opened July 17, 1983 at the People's Light and Theatre Company in Malvern, Pennsylvania under the direction of that company's artistic director, Danny Fruchter. The cast included Larry Block as Benny, Sherry Steiner as Norma, and Louis Lippa as Leo.

The first full-length version of the script, including material incorporated from *George's File,* opened on February 10, 1984 at the Hartford Stage Company. Emily Mann was once again the able director, and she and Hartford's artistic director, Mark Lamos, asked many questions which provoked significant additions. The cast reunited Larry Block as Benny and Robin Groves as Norma; Alvin Epstein played Leo.

The New York premiere opened on June 1, 1989 at the Vineyard Theatre (Doug Aibel, artistic director, Barbara Zinn Krieger, executive director and Jon Nakagawa, managing director) under the direction of Gloria Muzio and featured John Seitz as Benny, Ava Haddad as Norma and Stephen Pearlman as Leo.

A radio version, produced by Los Angeles Theatre Works (Susan Albert Loewenberg) was recorded in June, 1995 under the direction of Gordon Hunt and featured Garry Marshall as Benny, Sally Murphy as Norma and Hector Elizondo as Leo. (A cassette version of the broadcast is available for purchase at 1-800-708-8863.)

I go to pains to list all of the above because *The Value of Names,* though not radically revised or restructured, has benefitted from each of its presentations. Quite simply, were it not for the support of non-profit theatres, I doubt if this play would exist.

Jeffrey Sweet

THE VALUE OF NAMES

The set is a patio high up in hills over Malibu. Upstage is Benny Silverman's house. It is the house of someone very comfortably off. The patio may be entered either through a door from the house or through a gate that leads directly from the road.

At rise, Benny has an easel set up and is painting the view from his patio. He is in his late sixties or early seventies and appears to be in fine health. Norma is in her twenties. A few seconds of quiet, then he speaks —

BENNY. Does it sound too Jewish?
NORMA. *(To audience.)* No, hold on. First, a couple of things you should know: It's 1981. A patio up in the hills overlooking Malibu. Over there, the Pacific Ocean. Next to me, my father. On the whole, I have less trouble with the Pacific.
BENNY. *(As in "Are you finished?")* OK?
NORMA. Sure. Go ahead.
BENNY. Does it sound too Jewish?
NORMA. Pop —
BENNY. You're changing your name. Stands to reason there's something about the one you've got you don't like. Or maybe find inconvenient.
NORMA. *(To audience.)* I should have known he'd take it like this.
BENNY. Could put you at a disadvantage. A name like Silverman. Some parts — the casting directors won't even look at you. I know. Say, for instance, they do a new version of *The Bells of St. Mary's.* Casting people see the name Norma Silverman, what are they going to say? "Nope, don't call her. A person obviously without nun potential. Get me an O'Hara or a Kelly. Get away with this Silverman." And there goes your chance to

play Ingrid Bergman. Of course, Bergman, too, is a name that's a little suspect.

NORMA. Pop —

BENNY. But then, one look at her, that question's laid to rest. Even if she did play Golda Meir once. One look at that nose of hers. That was not a Jewish nose. But then — thanks to the magic of science — who can tell from a nose?

NORMA. Of course.

BENNY. I could show you Horowitzes and Steins and Margulieses with noses on them look like they belong to Smiths. Very funny seeing a Smith nose on a Horowitz. Or a Horowitz nose on a Smith, although this is rarer.

NORMA. They don't transplant noses.

BENNY. You want to know why?

NORMA. *(With a side-long look to the audience.)* OK, why?

BENNY. Run the risk of the body rejecting. Sure, it's a big problem. Heart transplant, kidney transplant — the body sometimes says, "No, thank you. Take it away." A case like that, all that happens is maybe someone dies. But a nose transplant — could you imagine the humiliation if that happened? Walking down the street, maybe you hiccup, a slight tearing sensation, and suddenly there's a draft in the middle of your face. You look down on the pavement, see two dainty nostrils staring up at Heaven.

NORMA. Are you finished?

BENNY. Are you?

NORMA. With what?

BENNY. This nonsense. This changing-your-name nonsense.

NORMA. It's not nonsense. I'm going to do it.

BENNY. Fine. So do it. So what do you want from me?

NORMA. I don't want from you. I just thought I should tell you.

BENNY. OK, you've told me. So what do you want me to say? You want me to say congratulations? Like you're having a baby — congratulations? You're having a new name — how wonderful! And who's the father of this new name? I know who the father of the old name is. I see him sometimes on the Late Show.

NORMA. OK, Pop.
BENNY. It's not OK. But never mind, we won't talk about it.
NORMA. Fat chance.
BENNY. So what else is new? A sex change?
NORMA. It doesn't have anything to do with Jewish or not Jewish.
BENNY. What *has* it to do with?
NORMA. You.
BENNY. Oh. *I'm* the "to-do-with"?
NORMA. Here we go.
BENNY. *I'm* the reason you're changing your name?
NORMA. Do you want me to explain now? Or shall I give you a little room for a tirade?
BENNY. What tirade?
NORMA. The tirade you're gearing up for.
BENNY. Who, me?
NORMA. I wish you'd understand.
BENNY. What's to understand? You're changing your name. You're changing your name because it's my name. This makes me feel instantly terrific and wonderful. It makes me feel how glad I am to have my daughter's love and respect. How fulfilling it is to be a parent. How worth it all it's all been. Would you like a little coffee?
NORMA. Look, every time I've ever done anything, every time I've ever been reviewed, they always put in that I'm your daughter. My name is not Norma Silverman. My name is Norma Silverman Benny Silverman's daughter.
BENNY. So what are you trying to do — convince people you're the product of a virgin birth?
NORMA. I'm very proud of being your daughter. But I would like, for once, when I get on a stage, for them to see me. Not just see you in me. There's a comparison implied there. "Is she as good as...?"
BENNY. Aren't you?
NORMA. I don't think I should have to fight that. You really don't want to understand, do you?
BENNY. Who put you up to this?
NORMA. What?

BENNY. This is your mother's idea, isn't it?
NORMA. No.
BENNY. I recognize the style.
NORMA. What do you mean?
BENNY. Right after the divorce, she got her driver's license changed back to her maiden name. Sarah Teitel. And her checking account and her magazine subscriptions and all the rest. Sarah Teitel. Didn't want to be known by her married name any more, thank you very much. Oh no. Said she wouldn't use it ever again. You know what I did? I made the alimony checks out to "Mrs. Benny Silverman." Would have loved to see her face when she had to endorse them.
NORMA. She didn't have anything to do with this.
BENNY. Maybe not, but she didn't tell you no.
NORMA. Actually, she told me you'd probably scream your head off, but she understood.
BENNY. That's generous of her.
NORMA. She respected my decision. Because that's what it was, Pop — my decision. She didn't enter into it. It's something I decided to do by myself, for myself. It's what I wanted.
BENNY. Fine — you wanted, you got.
NORMA. You know something — if you look at it the right way, it's a compliment.
BENNY. It is?
NORMA. If you look at it the right way.
BENNY. Let's hear this right way.
NORMA. Never mind.
BENNY. No compliment?
NORMA. Help.
BENNY. First it's out with the name, then it's good-bye compliment. Beats me why I should give you a cup of coffee.
NORMA. I don't want a cup of coffee.
BENNY. I can understand that. If I were you, I'd have enough trouble sleeping at night.
NORMA. *(Referring to the painting.)* I like it.
BENNY. Do you know anything about art?
NORMA. Do I have to know something about art to like it?
BENNY. If you knew something about art, you'd be able to

appreciate the shadings, the nuances — all the really subtle reasons why this is lousy.
NORMA. One of the things I love about you is this terrifically graceful way you have of accepting compliments.
BENNY. I like my compliments honest.
NORMA. What's not honest? I said I like it. I *do* like it. I didn't say that it's good.
BENNY. Oh, so you *don't* think it's good.
NORMA. Obviously I'm not entitled to think it's good *or* bad. I'm not even entitled to like it. So what *am* I entitled to? Statements of verifiable fact only? OK, a statement of verifiable fact: You are painting a painting, and it's sitting on an easel.
BENNY. Thank you, I'm flattered.
NORMA. And what would be so terrible if I liked it?
BENNY. Anybody can like. To like doesn't take any great skill, any great powers of discernment.
NORMA. I see. Only people with certifiably elevated taste are entitled to like something.
BENNY. Do you know what Monet or Chagall would say if they saw this?
NORMA. What?
BENNY. "Benny, stick to your acting."
NORMA. So why don't you?
BENNY. I like it.
NORMA. *You* like it?
BENNY. Yeah.
NORMA. I thought you said it's lousy.
BENNY. It *is* lousy.
NORMA. It's lousy but you like it.
BENNY. It's *because* I know that it's lousy I can like it.
NORMA. Come again?
BENNY. I don't pretend it's good. I don't delude myself. All I can say is that standing here, doing this, I enjoy myself. It doesn't have to be good for me to enjoy myself.
NORMA. Someone should make you a ride in an amusement park.
BENNY. You really like it?
NORMA. Yes.

BENNY. When I finish, it's yours. I hope you treat it better than other things I've given you. Like my name.
NORMA. OK, Pop —
BENNY. *(Referring to a playscript near her.)* I've read this script of yours.
NORMA. I didn't write it.
BENNY. Well, you're going to be in it.
NORMA. That still doesn't make it mine.
BENNY. It makes you associated with it.
NORMA. As in guilt by association?
BENNY. Who said anything about guilt?
NORMA. Your tone does. You don't like the play.
BENNY. It's OK for what it is. Are you really going to take off your clothes?
NORMA. Not clothes. Just my top.
BENNY. Your top isn't clothes?
NORMA. I'm not taking off my clothes, plural. I'm taking off a piece of clothing, singular.
BENNY. A piece of clothing singular, that covers up parts of you, plural.
NORMA. It's not a big deal. A lot of plays these days call for it.
BENNY. That excuses everything.
NORMA. I didn't realize there was anything to excuse.
BENNY. It's your business.
NORMA. It is, you know.
BENNY. You knew what was in the script before you signed the contract?
NORMA. Of course.
BENNY. It's your business. It's not my ass people will be looking at.
NORMA. It's not my ass either.
BENNY. Just your boobies.
NORMA. That's right.
BENNY. I never had to do that. Of course, who would pay to see my boobies? Or my ass, for that matter?
NORMA. Who knows, somebody might.
BENNY. Nobody I'd want to meet.

NORMA. I knew you were going to pick up on that. Out of everything in the script, that was the one element you were going to bring up.
BENNY. You like this play?
NORMA. I like it very much. I like my part very much. I feel very lucky to have landed it.
BENNY. All right.
NORMA. It's my business?
BENNY. Who else's?
NORMA. Not yours?
BENNY. Never.
NORMA. Well, I'm glad we got that settled.
BENNY. There was never any issue.
NORMA. Could have fooled me.
BENNY. And your mother?
NORMA. What about her?
BENNY. She doesn't have any opinion?
NORMA. All she wanted to know was if it's in —
BENNY and NORMA. *(Together.)* — good taste.
BENNY. Of course, I'm used to a different kind of play. The kind with ideas and metaphors.
NORMA. I think this play is metaphoric.
BENNY. There is nothing metaphoric about an attractive young woman with her top off.
NORMA. That moment you keep harping on is about vulnerability.
BENNY. In your mind it may be about vulnerability. Maybe in the playwright's mind. In the audience's mind it will be about tits. The women out there will be thinking, "Gee, I couldn't do that. Well, maybe I could do that. But how many margaritas would it take?" Meanwhile, the guys in the audience will be thinking — Well, you *know* what they'll be thinking. And their wives will know what they're thinking. And the women will look at their husbands like they're saying, "Yeah, and what are you gawking at?" And the guys will go, "Hey, I'm not gawking." And the women'll go, "Oh, yeah, right." And the guys will go, "Hey, but it's OK: this isn't tits, this is art. I'm having a catharsis here. Swear to God." You're up there acting your heart out, in the

meantime, they've forgotten your character's *name.*
NORMA. Could be the audience is more sophisticated than you think.
BENNY. Don't believe me then.
NORMA. It's not a question of my believing you or not. I believe that you see things the way you see things. I just don't. But things have changed in the theatre since you got started. I know it's hard to believe, Dad, but Clifford Odets is dead and gone.
BENNY. Clifford Odets? He was dead and gone even before he was dead.
NORMA. Maybe you'd like to recommend a good hotel.
BENNY. Hotel, for what?
NORMA. To stay in.
BENNY. You don't like the bed in your room?
NORMA. The bed's fine.
BENNY. I should hope so. The mattress was rated a "best buy" from *Consumer's Union.* What are you talking about a hotel? What have I got a house with three bedrooms for, so that you can pay money to strangers to sleep someplace?
NORMA. Look, the next few weeks aren't going to be easy for me. It's a new script, and what's undoubtedly going to happen is that, after I've finally memorized the lines, they're all going to be changed on me during rehearsal.
BENNY. That goes with the territory.
NORMA. What I'm concerned about is what goes with *this* territory. Staying here.
BENNY. A nice view of the Pacific where occasionally a whale swims by, spouts off.
NORMA. And you.
BENNY. I don't swim any more.
NORMA. You do your share of spouting off.
BENNY. That's me — Benny the whale. *(Benny laughs and goes back to his painting.)*
NORMA. *(To audience.)* I was fifteen years old, pushing a shopping cart at the A&P, when I found out what he'd been through. There were two people standing on line ahead of me, so I checked out the magazine rack to see what I could waste

a few minutes with. And there was a caricature of my father grinning out at me from the cover of *TV Guide.* At the bottom it said, "Benny Silverman of *Rich But Happy.*" That was the name of the situation comedy he played a crazy neighbor on — *Rich But Happy.* So, of course I'm eager to see what it has to say about him. Maybe he'll mention me or Mom, though at that point they'd been divorced already ten years or so. So I'm standing on line at the A&P, smiling, reading about how he's buddies with all the technicians on the set, about a practical joke he played on the producer once, about how the younger actors on the show revere him as a comic genius, and so forth and so on. And then there was this classic *TV Guide* transitional sentence. Something about — "But Benny Silverman still has vivid memories of the black days when his chief concern was not fine-tuning a laugh but fighting for the right to practice his craft." This was followed by how he was named in front of the House Committee on Un-American Activities. And how he had been subpoenaed to appear, and how he did appear but did not cooperate. And then, years of not being able to find work. I was in the middle of this when it was my turn at the check-out counter. I paid for the groceries, and I took them home and dumped them on the kitchen table. And I asked my mother whether it had been by planning or oversight that nobody had ever told me a word about it.

BENNY. Planning. I asked her not to.

NORMA. Why?

BENNY. It happened before you were born. It had nothing to do with you. Why should you be bothered by it?

NORMA. You expected me never to find out?

BENNY. What did it matter whether you found out or not?

NORMA. If it didn't matter, why keep it from me?

BENNY. You were a kid. Your mother and I figured, between homework and puberty, you had enough to handle. What did you need to know about something that took place years before you were even conceived?

NORMA. It might have helped me to understand you better.

BENNY. Understand what?

NORMA. Why you are what you are. Why you do what you do.

BENNY. You expect to understand all that? Nothing like modest ambitions.
NORMA. I had to go to the library, for God's sake. I had to look up your name in indexes. I had to *read* about you.
BENNY. Well, at least some good came of it. It was always murder to get you to crack a book.
NORMA. Can I ask you something?
BENNY. No. What is it?
NORMA. There was another book I found, on political theatre. And there was a picture. A photo of the Labor Players —
BENNY. *(Correcting.)* The *New* Labor Players.
NORMA. Maybe seven or eight of you in the picture. And standing next to you is Leo Greshen, and your arm is around his shoulder.
BENNY. That was a fake arm. They touched that arm into the picture.
NORMA. He was a friend of yours.
BENNY. He gave that appearance for a while.
NORMA. So what did he say?
BENNY. Look it up. The transcript's public, it's easy to find.
NORMA. I don't mean his testimony. I mean what did he say to you?
BENNY. Why you want to dig into this is beyond —
NORMA. Did he call you afterwards? Try to explain?
BENNY. Not afterwards, before. Squealer's etiquette. Sort of like an arsonist calling up ahead of time. "Hello, I'm going to burn your house down. Thought you might like to know." Only instead — "Hello, I'm going to burn your career down." "Thanks a lot, Leo. Hope to return the favor someday."
NORMA. But he was a friend. Didn't he give you reasons?
BENNY. Oh, everybody knew the reasons why. He had the prospect of directing his first picture, and he didn't want this to blow it for him.
NORMA. He said this to you? That was why he was going to testify?
BENNY. Did you know "testify" and "testimony" come from the same Latin root as "testes" as in "balls"? I'm not making this up. In Rome, if you wanted to make a big point that something

you said was true, when you said it, you'd grab your balls. Which is why I don't think what he said to the Committee really qualifies as testimony. How could it? The man had no balls to grab.

NORMA. I shouldn't have had to find out that way — reading it in a book.

BENNY. "Find out." You talk as if you'd uncovered something shameful.

NORMA. Being ashamed of something is one reason why someone may keep something secret.

BENNY. I was not ashamed. I *am* not ashamed. Perhaps I had a very good reason for not telling you.

NORMA. Such as what?

BENNY. To protect you.

NORMA. To protect me from something you weren't ashamed of. Sure, that makes sense.

BENNY. Do you remember the Epsteins?

NORMA. The Epsteins?

BENNY. The Epsteins, the Epsteins.

NORMA. Why?

BENNY. Do you?

NORMA. I think so.

BENNY. They lived in your aunt Bertha's building.

NORMA. All right, yes, I remember the Epsteins. So?

BENNY. All right. One night, your mother and I were at the Epsteins'. Ten-thirty, eleven o'clock, their daughter Becky comes in. She's coming home from a date with someone her parents don't approve of, which is to say someone who isn't Jewish. An argument starts. Didn't they tell Becky not to see him? She doesn't care what they told her. She has a mind of her own, her own life to lead, she'll make her own decisions, etc. If she wants to go out with him she'll go out with him, and it's just too damn bad if her parents don't like it. And it keeps going like this, back and forth, more and more heat and passion and arm waving. Finally, her mother cries out, "This is what I survived Buchenwald for? For a daughter with a mouth like this?" I shudder to think how much time that girl probably ended up spending on a psychiatrist's couch.

NORMA. So you think they shouldn't have told her?
BENNY. I think it's not right to bludgeon other people with your suffering.
NORMA. There's a difference between bludgeoning and telling.
BENNY. There's a difference between everything and everything else. You can draw distinctions till you're blue in the face.
NORMA. Don't dance away from me like that. We're talking about something here.
BENNY. All right, so I was a little over-protective. When did this become a felony? But what did you learn that was so valuable? That some son-of-a-bitch, in order to save his own ass, got up in front of some other sons-of-bitches and said he'd seen me a handful of times in the same room with another group of sons-of-bitches.
NORMA. And you didn't work for years after that.
BENNY. This was all way before you were born. Do you ever remember going to bed hungry because I couldn't provide? No. So it didn't touch you. So why are you complaining? Are you complaining because you didn't have pain? Or are you complaining because the pain you did have isn't the pain you wanted to have? Maybe you can give Becky Epstein a call, see if she wants to trade. Or maybe she'll give you the name of her shrink. You can go lie on his couch and complain about how awful I was that I didn't lift up my shirt and show you ancient scars.
NORMA. Just because I didn't know about it doesn't mean that it hasn't touched me.
BENNY. Enough already. Are we going to go over all this again? *(A beat.)* So, what name now? So when I look in the program I know which one is you.
NORMA. Norma Teitel.
BENNY. Teitel? *(Norma nods.)* I should have guessed. You sure this wasn't your mother's idea? *(A beat.)*
NORMA. Hey, are you glad I'm here?
BENNY. How could you doubt? *(They both smile. During Norma's following speech, Benny hauls his easel and canvas and paint into the house. He is back on the patio at the conclusion of the speech.)*

NORMA. *(To audience.)* And you know something? We get along OK for a little over a week. And the play's coming along well, too. And then our director has a stroke. They take him off to the hospital, where they tell us the prognosis is, thank God, good. But that leaves us without a director. The producers call a hiatus for a couple of days so they can put their heads together and come up with a new director. And then I get a call and they tell me who they've decided on. And that their offer has been made and accepted. I tell them I have some problems with their choice. I explain why. They say they hope I will stay with the show, but that I have to decide quickly. "Think about it seriously," they say. I promise I will. And then I tell Pop.

BENNY. Do you tell me because you want my advice?

NORMA. I tell you because I think you should know. I mean, it's partially for your sake I'd be doing it. If I did it.

BENNY. Quitting?

NORMA. Yes.

BENNY. Well, it *is* your decision.

NORMA. I know.

BENNY. I will only say one thing, and this is not to in any way influence your decision, but — if you were to stay with the play, I wouldn't be able to go to it.

NORMA. You hate him that much?

BENNY. I used to go to see his stuff. And when it was good work, I'd be angry. And when it was bad or flopped, I'd get satisfaction. And then I thought to myself, "What am I doing to myself? I mean, this is stupid. I've got myself to the point where I'm happy about bad work and miserable about successes." I was letting the guy twist me into knots, plus a percentage of my ticket money was going into his pocket so that I was paying for him to do this to me. So I stopped. I don't go to see his stuff, I don't go to see the stuff of some of the others. And do you know something? The world doesn't end because I miss a play or a movie.

NORMA. So there are people whose work you won't go to see.

BENNY. I think that's what I said.

NORMA. Because of their political beliefs?

BENNY. Because of the way they *expressed* these beliefs.

NORMA. I guess you wouldn't work with them either.
BENNY. No, I wouldn't.
NORMA. When you were on *Rich But Happy*, did the issue ever come up? Was there ever a time when the producer wanted to hire one of these guys that you wouldn't work with?
BENNY. No, they knew not to do that.
NORMA. They knew there were certain people you didn't want hired.
BENNY. They were sensitive to the way I felt.
NORMA. Was there a list?
BENNY. What?
NORMA. Of people you wouldn't work with. Did you write up a list? *(A beat.)*
BENNY. Cute.
NORMA. Well, I'm your daughter.
BENNY. What you're describing is not the same.
NORMA. You weren't hired, and you turned around and saw to it that other people weren't hired.
BENNY. There's a difference. There's a distinction.
NORMA. I'm sure there is.
BENNY. To anybody with a pair of eyes in her head.
NORMA. Explain the distinction to me.
BENNY. I don't have to defend myself to you.
NORMA. All right.
BENNY. What — do you think I should forget? Would you expect me to work with, for instance, a Nazi?
NORMA. Nazi?
BENNY. You know from Nazis, don't you? They're the guys who had the franchise on swastikas before the Hell's Angels. Let's say I'm in a movie, OK? I'm going to do a scene with this guy. While we're waiting to shoot, we're sitting around, we're kibbitzing. I tell an anecdote. He laughs and says, "You know that reminds me of something funny that happened when I was in the S.S."
NORMA. Right.
BENNY. So according to you what I should say back is "Hey, Fritz, want me to cue you on your lines?"
NORMA. Why is it whenever you get mad, you reach for a

Nazi?
BENNY. What are you talking about, "reach for a Nazi?"
NORMA. You do, you know.
BENNY. You make it sound like a soft drink. "Worked up a thirst? Reach for a nice, refreshing Nazi!"
NORMA. It's like a conversational pre-emptive strike. Whenever you don't agree with me, it always comes around to Nazis or anti-Semitism. First is my name too Jewish. Then it's Becky Epstein and the Holocaust. And now, even this, in come the jackboots again.
BENNY. "Even this?" What "this" are you saying "even this" about?
NORMA. McCarthyism, the blacklist —
BENNY. And you don't think that was anti-Semitism? Look at who was on the Committee. Martin Dies. Harold Velde. Karl Mundt.
NORMA. Oh come on, everybody with a German name isn't an anti-Semite. Besides which, there were a lot of people on the Committee who weren't German.
BENNY. That's right, Nixon isn't German. And we all know what a warm feeling he has for people of — how would he put it? — Hebraic persuasion? And as for the guys he and his buddies went after —
NORMA. All Jews, right?
BENNY. Let's just say you wouldn't have had trouble raising a minyan. Oh, and the fun the Committee had with the Jewish names! You can't tell from reading the transcripts — how they punched them, mis-pronounced them, tried to make them sound sinister and alien. "Carnovsky, Papirofsky, Ruskin." Ever hear anything so suspicious in your life? And did they have a field day with the ones who had *changed* their names! "You call yourself 'Holliday' but your real name, the name you were born with is what? 'Tuvim.'" As if they were talking to a criminal trying to hide something. You're going to tell me that wasn't anti-Semitism?
NORMA. That's not my point.
BENNY. Oh, I know what your point is.
NORMA. I never said you should work with Nazis.

BENNY. So, it's OK with you if I don't? I mean, you won't disapprove if I turn down a contract to co-star with Dr. Mengele?
NORMA. There *is* a difference between Mengele and Nixon.
BENNY. You're absolutely right — one murdered Jews, the other only made it hard for them to eat.
NORMA. OK, go ahead, twist everything.
BENNY. And you weren't twisting? That comment about my having a list?
NORMA. I was just raising what I thought was an interesting question.
BENNY. I was kept from working because some of the views I used to have suddenly weren't popular any more. If I prefer not to work with people who kept me from working or gave support to people who kept me from working, I think I'm within my rights. *(He exits into the house.)*
NORMA. Pop … *(She follows him off, hoping to calm him down. A second after she exits, Leo enters. Like Benny, he is in his late sixties, early seventies. He looks around the patio. He knows he is trespassing, but he is mentally prepared to face whoever might come out and face him. He is "casing" the place, when Norma returns to the patio. Initially, due to where he stands, she doesn't see him.)*
LEO. Miss Teitel? *(Startled, she turns to look at him.)*
NORMA. You're Leo Greshen.
LEO. *(With a smile.)* Guilty. I thought, rather than ring the doorbell, I'd just come around. I hope you don't mind.
NORMA. They told you.
LEO. Our beloved producers? Yes. At first, I couldn't figure it out. They said your father was somebody I used to know and that that was the reason why. And I kept thinking, "Teitel. When did I ever know a guy named Teitel?"
NORMA. My mother's name.
LEO. You changed it from Silverman?
NORMA. Yes.
LEO. Benny must love that. Why?
NORMA. Personal reasons.
LEO. You and he have a falling out?
NORMA. No.
LEO. OK.

NORMA. This is his house. I'm staying here.
LEO. Point taken.
NORMA. I shouldn't have said anything to them.
LEO. Them meaning our producers?
NORMA. I shouldn't have told them.
LEO. What then? Just walked out without warning?
NORMA. Of course not. I haven't decided to leave. All I said to them was that I was thinking about it. It didn't occur to me that they'd tell you.
LEO. Not to mention my popping up unannounced.
NORMA. There's the telephone.
LEO. True, but I've heard that the view here is terrific.
NORMA. Yes, well, there it is.
LEO. Very pretty.
NORMA. The blue part is the Pacific.
LEO. Somehow I never could live in LA. Oh, I usually have a good time here. But I'm really a lazy bastard at heart, and this climate would probably aggravate that. Too easy to forget that time is passing when there's basically only one season. You're from the East, too, aren't you?
NORMA. New York.
LEO. Sure, you know what I mean. Every three months, you've got another season kicking you in the ass, telling you that the meter's ticking. One moment you're trying to find your sandals, the next you're digging galoshes out from the closet. Keeps you alert. *(A beat.)* Is he here?
NORMA. Inside. Probably taking a nap.
LEO. Ah. *(A beat.)* Did he ask you to drop out?
NORMA. No.
LEO. But he's not terribly happy about it. About the idea of you working with me.
NORMA. Did you think he would be?
LEO. How is he anyway?
NORMA. Fine.
LEO. He's a talented man, your father. We did a lot of work together.
NORMA. I know.
LEO. He told you?

NORMA. Not really. I did some reading.
LEO. Reading?
NORMA. Yes.
LEO. What did he do — hand you a bibliography and tell you there'd be a quiz?
NORMA. There are certain things he just never talks about.
LEO. And I'm one of those things. Right. *(A beat.)* You know, there were once these two guys named Stalin and Trotsky. They were both bigwigs in the Russian revolution.
NORMA. You don't have to patronize me, Mr. Greshen. I do know who Stalin and Trotsky were.
LEO. In my experience, that puts you firmly in the minority of the people your age. Their idea of history is when the Beatles first appeared on Ed Sullivan. Anyway, as you apparently know, after Lenin died, Stalin took over and tossed Trotsky out of Russia. Parenthetically, Trotsky was later murdered with a pickax. One of these days Brian de Palma will make a movie about this. Anyway, if you were an earnest young student of history while Stalin was in power — at Moscow U., say, or Petrograd Prep — you would have searched in vain to find any mention of Trotsky's part in the revolution in the state-approved texts. In the jargon of the time, he became a non-person.
NORMA. Your point is?
LEO. Your father has the making of a fine Stalinist historian. Never talks about me at all, hunh?
NORMA. A little — recently, when I asked him. But not very much. The subject's painful for him, I guess.
LEO. Believe it or not, there was a time when he didn't hate my guts. But I don't imagine that was in your reading.
NORMA. You were both members of the New Labor Players.
LEO. Actually, I was one of the founders. A fellow named Mort Kessler was one of the other actors. He also wrote a lot of stuff. That's how he got started as a writer. Anyway, one day he brought in this piece — it was about St. Peter and about how two or three fat-cats con their way past him into Heaven. *(Remembering title.) Capitalist Heaven* — that's what we called it! Well, of course, as capitalists always did in our subtle little plays, they set up an exploitive society — turned the poor cherubim

into wage slaves in the harp factory, clipped their wings, etc. Anyway, we didn't have a St. Peter, and somebody knew your father. They had seen him do imitations or something at a party. So I met him. He was working in the garment district. I suggested he might have more fun earning next-to-nothing with us than earning almost-next-to-nothing hauling around big rolls of fabric. He believed me. And that's how he became an actor. He was a terrific St. Peter. Who would have guessed he would end up in a swanky place like this? Talk about "Capitalist Heaven." *(A beat.)*

NORMA. Did you want to see him?

LEO. I came out to see you.

NORMA. Yes, but this is his house. You must have known there was a reasonable chance of running into him.

LEO. I'm not afraid of that.

NORMA. I didn't say you were.

LEO. I'd like you to stay with the show.

NORMA. Have you seen any of my work?

LEO. The producers seem to think you're good.

NORMA. But you've never seen me do anything?

LEO. Nope.

NORMA. If I were to leave, it wouldn't be difficult for you to find someone else.

LEO. That's true.

NORMA. There are lots of good actresses.

LEO. A dozen or so at least.

NORMA. It might be easier for you.

LEO. Thank you for your concern, but I think I could bear up. I long ago accepted the fact that Mother Teresa would beat me in a popularity contest.

NORMA. I don't see why it would be worth it to you.

LEO. Why is your understanding so important?

NORMA. Because, if I were to stay, I'd like to know on what basis.

LEO. That you do your job. What other basis is there? You fulfill a contract that was negotiated in good faith. Or don't you think you can play the part?

NORMA. I can play it.

LEO. It's not unheard of for an actor to come up with a convenient excuse to leave if he thinks he's out of his depth.
NORMA. I can play the part.
LEO. I believe you. Now, as for me, you acknowledge that I probably can do that job I've been hired for. True?
NORMA. Yes.
LEO. Then isn't that all we need be concerned about?
NORMA. I should just do my work and go on about my business.
LEO. It's called a professional attitude.
NORMA. You wouldn't be trying to prove something to my father?
LEO. What would I be trying to prove?
NORMA. You can't tell me the fact that I'm his daughter doesn't enter into this somewhere. Let's face it, I'm being kind of difficult here. And it's not as if I have any real reputation or name that you should have to put up with it.
LEO. Wait a second. Do you want me to fire you?
NORMA. I didn't say that.
LEO. What do you want?
NORMA. Mr. Greshen, I happen to believe I'm good at what I do. I happen also to have a well-known father who's also an actor.
LEO. That can be an advantage.
NORMA. It's an advantage I don't want. Whatever my career is, wherever it goes, I want it to be on the basis of what I do myself. One of the real kicks of getting this part was that they hired me without knowing who my dad is. I mean, they hired *me*.
LEO. I understand.
NORMA. Well, now I get the feeling that it's because of him you want me to stay.
LEO. Isn't it because of him you're thinking of leaving?
NORMA. Those are two separate issues.
LEO. I don't think so.
NORMA. But it *is* because of him you want me to stay. At least partially.
LEO. If you've got to know, it's because I don't like being

walked out on. All right? *(A beat.)* Jesus, even if I *didn't* know you're Benny's daughter, I'd probably guess. You're a lot like him, Miss Teitel. By the way, that's a compliment. *(Benny enters. At first, Norma sees him and Leo doesn't. Then Leo senses his presence and turns around.)*

BENNY. Very difficult to nap. All this back and forth outside my window.

LEO. Hello, Benny.

BENNY. She's right, you know.

LEO. Oh?

BENNY. If you think you're going to prove something to me —

LEO. No?

BENNY. You proved all that you had to prove to me a long time ago. That fabulous phone call.

LEO. The book is closed, hunh?

BENNY. That's the way it is.

LEO. You know, I've got an aunt Sadie, still has my cousin Ernie's baby shoes. A friend of mine, he saves matchbooks from restaurants. But you — you collect old injuries.

BENNY. A shame, isn't it?

LEO. I think so.

BENNY. A shame and a waste. You feel sorry for me.

LEO. I do.

BENNY. I am touched by your concern.

LEO. I can tell.

BENNY. No, really. It comes a little late. But what's thirty years in the grand scheme of things?

LEO. I've always been concerned.

BENNY. "'I weep for you,' the Walrus said, 'I deeply sympathize.'" You know, I believe him. I believe his tears are genuine. I have my doubts about the Carpenter, but the Walrus is a feeling man. Or as feeling as a Walrus can be. You, too, Leo.

LEO. Same old Benny.

BENNY. Some people are born walrus, some people achieve walrus, and some have walrus thrust upon them. You can't blame the people who are *born* walrus. After all, that's all they know. But the ones who *choose* it —

LEO. It's all nice and simple for you, isn't it?
BENNY. Why don't I throw you off my patio?
LEO. Maybe you don't want to.
BENNY. Why wouldn't I want to?
LEO. It's been almost thirty years.
BENNY. You say that as if there's a statute of limitations.
LEO. *Are* you going to throw me off your patio?
BENNY. I'm thinking about it. *(A beat.)* You want a beer?
LEO. Couldn't hurt.
BENNY. *(To Norma.)* You want to bring this bastard a beer?
NORMA. What about you?
BENNY. Why not? *(Norma exits. Leo sits. Benny picks up a bowl of chips, offers him some. Leo takes a few. Benny grabs some chips for himself and sits. For a while, they sit and munch chips in silence. Then —)*
LEO. She looks like her mother.
BENNY. We're divorced.
LEO. I heard. I'm sorry.
BENNY. She isn't. She's a very happy divorcee. She's told me so herself. *(A beat.)* So you're coming back to the theatre. What happened? The movies go sour on you?
LEO. The movies are going fine. As a matter of a fact, in a couple months I start a new one.
BENNY. But you're directing this play.
LEO. I wasn't aware of any rule that if you do one you can't do the other. *(Norma returns with two beers. She hands one to Leo during the following. He nods thanks.)* No, the producers were in a bind. They needed a director. They talked to my agent. The timing worked out OK. I read the script. *(Norma now hands Benny his beer.)*
BENNY. You like it?
LEO. It's a little lighter than I usually do, but I thought it might be fun to direct.
BENNY. Fun to look at my daughter's chest? *(Norma wishes the ground would open up.)*
LEO. Hunh?
BENNY. The scene she takes her top off.
LEO. Oh that.

BENNY. Yes, that.
LEO. I told the playwright I want to cut that. I don't like naked actors on the stage. Distracts from the play.
BENNY. Oh.
LEO. You don't agree? *(Benny shrugs, but he sends a pointed look in Norma's direction.)*
NORMA. I think I'm going to take a drive.
BENNY. Where to?
NORMA. Nowhere in particular. Just a drive. Things to think about.
BENNY. I see.
NORMA. Besides, you probably want to be alone, right?
BENNY. *(Not replying to her line.)* Will you be gone long?
NORMA. I don't know.
LEO. I'm glad I had a chance to meet you, Miss Teitel.
NORMA. Mr. Greshen. *(She exits.)*
LEO. You should let her do the play, Benny. It's a good part. People will notice. She'll be on her way. *(Benny laughs.)* What?
BENNY. Good thing you didn't say that in front of her.
LEO. What?
BENNY. About my "letting" her. She would have laughed in your face.
LEO. Is that so?
BENNY. The idea that I have anything to do with what she decides.
LEO. Not a thing, hunh?
BENNY. Do you think I "let" her go into acting?
LEO. No?
BENNY. If you knew how hard I tried to keep her out of this business. And you can see how successful I was.
LEO. She never consults you.
BENNY. Who's around to consult? This is the first time we've actually laid eyes on each other in almost two years. She's in New York, I'm here.
LEO. And the telephone hasn't been invented.
BENNY. Why should she care about my opinion?
LEO. *(Anticipating Benny saying this —)* You're just her father.
BENNY. What do you think? She does your show, I'm going

to cut her out of my will?

LEO. Apart from everything else, whether or not the show does well, I think she'd find it a valuable experience.

BENNY. You want me to tell her that? You want me to put in a good word for you, Leo? *(A beat.)*

LEO. When's the last time *you* did a play?

BENNY. Half dozen years ago.

LEO. Which?

BENNY. *Front Page.*

LEO. Who'd you play?

BENNY. Pincus.

LEO. Remind me.

BENNY. The little schmuck with the message from the Governor.

LEO. Bet you were good.

BENNY. Me? I was terrific.

LEO. Not a big part, though.

BENNY. It was one of those all-star casts. Limited run.

LEO. Ah.

BENNY. I did it for the fun of it.

LEO. Was it fun?

BENNY. Sure.

LEO. So why not anything since?

BENNY. Wasn't *that* much fun.

LEO. Oh.

BENNY. Besides, nobody's sent me a script I really wanted to do in a long time. God, the things they call musicals these days! Most of them seem to be about some kid screaming how he wants to be a star. I've also been sent a lot of plays about people dying. You think they're trying to tell me something? Sometimes you get an adventurous blend of the two — about celebrities who die. From what I can tell, nobody's writing about anything anymore but show business and cancer. As if there were a difference.

LEO. You don't think you're overstating the case?

BENNY. Not by much, no.

LEO. You could always revive *Capitalist Heaven.*

BENNY. At least that was about something.

LEO. Yeah, about twenty-five minutes.
BENNY. You didn't think so at the time.
LEO. At the time was at the time.
BENNY. What a way with words you have!
LEO. We were talking about you doing a play.
BENNY. Why should I haul my ass down to some drafty theatre eight times a week? It's not like I need the money.
LEO. That I noticed. *(Referring to the house.)* Is the inside as nice as the outside?
BENNY. You'll have to take my word. *(A beat.)*
LEO. When did you start painting?
BENNY. How do you know I'm painting?
LEO. I could pretend to be Sherlock Holmes and say it's the smudge of blue on the side of your thumb.
BENNY. Did Norma tell you?
LEO. Nobody told me. I saw.
BENNY. Saw what?
LEO. One of your paintings.
BENNY. Where?
LEO. I was at someone's house. There was a picture on the wall. A view from this patio.
BENNY. I paint it a lot. Monet had water lilies and haystacks. Silverman's got smog.
LEO. Anyway, I told him I liked it, and he said you painted it.
BENNY. He?
LEO. Mort Kessler.
BENNY. I didn't know you and Morty were in touch.
LEO. More than in touch.
BENNY. Oh?
LEO. We get together whenever I'm out here. Or he gives me a call when he's east. Sure.
BENNY. From what happened I wouldn't say it was all that sure.
LEO. Oh, we patched all that up a long time ago.
BENNY. Patched it up?
LEO. There was a fund-raiser. Somebody did a dinner in their home, for the farmworkers, I think. One of those, I don't

know. As it happened, Morty and I found ourselves seated near each other. He pretended I wasn't there for a while. Then I remember some woman walked by with impossibly blonde hair. Well, the lady I was with made some comment like, "Do you believe that hair?" And Morty said, "Hey, I happen to know her mother was a natural fluorescent." I laughed. He looked at me. You can't ignore a man who laughs at your joke, right? And we started talking, and before the evening was over we were friends again.

BENNY. He never said.

LEO. Probably thought it would upset you.

BENNY. Why should it upset me who he chooses for friends? Just surprises me a little, that's all.

LEO. Like I said, we patched it up.

BENNY. He always did have a forgiving streak. You know, a couple weeks ago, I even heard him say something nice about his third wife.

LEO. He didn't forgive me. I didn't ask him to forgive me. I don't ask anybody to forgive me.

BENNY. He may have done it without your asking. Without your permission. He's got a sneaky side.

LEO. I don't think so. I don't think forgiving had anything to do with anything. I think he just put it aside. Somewhere along the line, he must have weighed things in the balance —

BENNY. And put it aside.

LEO. Yeah.

BENNY. First he weighed it, then he patched it, then he put it aside. Where? In storage?

LEO. In the past, where it belongs.

BENNY. Well, he never told me.

LEO. He knows you had strong feelings.

BENNY. I still do.

LEO. I guessed as much. But I suppose you're entitled.

BENNY. Thank you. *(A beat.)*

LEO. So, how are you feeling?

BENNY. How am I feeling about what?

LEO. The question is health, Benny, not opinions.

BENNY. I'm feeling fine.

LEO. You've recovered.
BENNY. What am I supposed to have recovered from?
LEO. Morty said something about you in the hospital.
BENNY. Oh, that. Nothing dramatic. Just a little prostate trouble.
LEO. How much is a little?
BENNY. It got to the point where it was taking more time for me to pee than to prepare my taxes. The doctor kind of thought maybe we should do something about that. So did my accountant.
LEO. So you went to the hospital. How was that?
BENNY. Not too terrible actually.
LEO. Did they knock you out?
BENNY. No. They gave me a spinal. That just anesthetizes you from about the navel down. The upper part stays wide awake. As a matter of a fact, they asked me did I want to watch?
LEO. And?
BENNY. I took a pass.
LEO. If you could take a pass, you wouldn't have needed the operation.
BENNY. Anyway, I said no, thanks, my idea of entertainment was not to watch them drill for oil in my privates. So they put up a sheet to block the view, and they called in a Roto Rooter man. A few hours, and that was it.
LEO. So it was all right.
BENNY. All right? What are you talking about? Better than all right! Fantastic! Really, Leo, you should give it a try.
LEO. I mean it healed nicely. No complications.
BENNY. Such an interest you take! What — you want to make an on-site inspection?
LEO. Maybe some other time.
BENNY. Nope, you had your chance. For a while there I had to avoid orange juice, grapefruit juice, pineapples —
LEO. Why?
BENNY. Citric acid, you know. Stings like crazy.
LEO. Right.
BENNY. But it's fine now.
LEO. Well, that's good news.

BENNY. Jesus.
LEO. What?
BENNY. I remember when we used to talk about girls and the revolution. Now —
LEO. You want to talk about girls, I'll be glad to talk about girls.
BENNY. Morty keeps you posted on my health.
LEO. He doesn't hand me bulletins or anything, but I like to keep track of the old gang.
BENNY. You heard about George.
LEO. I saw it in the *Times*. Christ, every morning, opening the goddamned *Times* to find out who I've survived.
BENNY. I know.
LEO. You went to the funeral?
BENNY. They didn't have a formal funeral. There was a kind of memorial thing.
LEO. What was that like?
BENNY. Sort of fun actually. Everybody got up, told stories.
LEO. *(Laughing.)* Oh?
BENNY. No, the clean ones.
LEO. Must have been a short memorial.
BENNY. They read some from his file. You know, he got the stuff the FBI kept on him under the Freedom of Information thing.
LEO. Sounds like a lot of laughs.
BENNY. Did you ever hear about when he was in the army?
LEO. I know that he was in the army —
BENNY. About when he was in the hospital in the army?
LEO. Wait a second? About the FBI agent?
BENNY. Came to question the other guys in the ward about him —
LEO. I've heard it, yeah.
BENNY. Didn't recognize him. Gave a testimonial to his own —
LEO. Yeah, I heard it.
BENNY. They asked him his name —
BENNY and LEO. Jake Barnes.
BENNY. You heard it.

LEO. I heard it.
BENNY. You ever send for your file?
LEO. What for?
BENNY. To see what they said about you.
LEO. What for?
BENNY. I sent for mine.
LEO. To see what "they" said about you?
BENNY. What are you smiling about?
LEO. You remember the end of the second part of *Faust?*
BENNY. It doesn't spring to my lips, no.
LEO. Goethe.
BENNY. All of a sudden this is *G.E. College Bowl.*
LEO. He talks about "the Eternal Feminine." The last line is something about constantly pursuing "the Eternal Feminine."
BENNY. So?
LEO. So, instead of "the Eternal Feminine," for you it's "the Eternal They." "They" do this, "they" keep you from doing that. Always "they."
BENNY. Not always, Leo. Sometimes it's "you."
LEO. So you sent for your file.
BENNY. I sent for my file.
LEO. Anything interesting?
BENNY. Great nostalgia value. Lists of the petitions I signed, the magazines I subscribed to. Some bastard even showed up at one of the benefits I performed at. "Subject performed allegedly humorous routine — "
LEO. "Allegedly humorous." He said that?
BENNY. Fucking critics, they're everywhere. You remember — just after Sarah and I got married, I had to go out of town on that tour?
LEO. *Native Son*, wasn't it?
BENNY. Probably. Anyway, Sarah was doing real well in radio then, so she didn't go out with me. So we wrote each other a lot. Some of it was kind of personal stuff.
LEO. You mean love letters?
BENNY. Well, yeah, I guess you could call them that. Anyway, I'd lost the originals a long time ago in one of our moves. But, like I say, I had the FBI send me my file, and they must have

kept a mail cover on us, because there they were — all the letters I'd lost. A lot of them anyway.

LEO. They Xeroxed your letters?

BENNY. Xeroxed? In nineteen-forty —

LEO. Right.

BENNY. No, someone actually typed them up. Probably anchored them with a book or something so they'd lie flat, be easier to type from. You know Sarah's handwriting — probably had to hire a cryptographer to decipher. Sarah and I were waiting for the final divorce papers when I got that file from the Feds. *(A beat.)* I almost sent her copies.

LEO. *(Gently.)* Almost?

BENNY. What purpose would it have served? It was all over between us by then.

LEO. Benny, what happened?

BENNY. Well —

LEO. The two of you — I've never seen a couple like — *(Benny suddenly realizes how close he's gotten to the old friendship. He forces himself to pull back.)*

BENNY. No, I'm not going to talk about that.

LEO. If there's something you want to —

BENNY. Not with you. *(A beat.)*

LEO. OK.

BENNY. Anyway, I get some satisfaction out of knowing that the S.O.B. who typed that all up is probably dead now.

LEO. Or maybe having a prostate operation of his own.

BENNY. He should only have it done without a spinal. *(A beat.)* How's your beer?

LEO. Fine. *(A beat.)* I was given an honorary degree, you know. Last spring.

BENNY. In what — communications?

LEO. A doctor of letters, actually. Avery College, New Hampshire. For my body of work. That's how they phrased it. Sounds cadaverous, doesn't it? "Here lies Leo Greshen's body of work." I had to laugh when I was told. But I said sure. Sure, I'd be honored to be honored. And, generous fellow, that I am, I say I'll throw in a seminar on directing or some damn thing. They couldn't be happier. I'm met at the airport. I have dinner with a bunch of deans and professors and nice faculty wives, faculty husbands, whatever. Some nice stroking. Springtime in New Hampshire. Who could object to that? So I'm scheduled to speak to this media studies class. The guy who runs the class introduces me. My pictures, the plays I've directed, blah, blah, blah, and would you please welcome. Applause. All very nice. He asks me questions. I answer. I make jokes. He tosses in a quip or two like a regular Dick Cavett. Everything's bopping along well. About forty-five minutes of this, he says he's going to open the floor to questions. Four or five hands shoot up. I see this one intent kid off to the side, near the window. Skinny kid with eyes like lasers. I look at him and I know he's going to ask it. I just know it. But my friend, the would-be Dick Cavett, calls on some girl who asks me how it was to work with so-and-so, and I tell an amusing story and everybody laughs in the right place except for the kid with the laser eyes. I've barely finished my amusing story when his hand shoots up again. The professor again chooses another hand. Bearded kid wants to know if I story-board when I'm in pre-production. I tell another amusing story. Soon as I'm finished with that one, again that kid's hand shoots up. Again my host chooses another hand, but I interrupt him. I say, "Wait a second. There's a young man over there by the window seems to have something urgent to ask. Yes, son, what is it?" Yes, son, I'm thinking, go ahead and prove how brave and liberal you are. Nail me in front of all your nice classmates and your nice teacher on this nice, nice campus in New Hampshire. "Yes, son," I say, "what's your question?" He doesn't disappoint. No sooner has he said the magic words "House Committee on Un-American Activities" than my friend the professor interrupts, says that we are not here to discuss that. "We are here to discuss Mr. Greshen's art, Mr. Greshen's craft. We are here to learn what we can from Mr. Greshen's years of experience in the theatre and film. Politics has nothing to do with it." And he asks if there are any other questions. I answer two more, and my friend the professor wraps it up by thanking me on behalf of the class for my generosity and candor. Applause. My host and I go to the faculty lounge. He buys me a drink and tells me that he's sorry about the boy's rudeness. Apparently that boy has a habit of stirring things up. And that was why my friend hadn't wanted to call on him. He was trying to protect me. Seems like this kid had circulated a petition calling on the college to rescind the honorary degree. That it would not redound to the school's credit to honor a stoolie. This was not quite how my friend put it, but that was the gist of it. So there was a ceremony, I got my degree, shook a lot of nice hands and went home. And all through this I was thinking of how I should have answered the little bastard.

BENNY. And what would you have said?

LEO. That he hadn't earned the right to ask me that question. He hadn't earned the right to brandish his moral indignation in my face.

BENNY. That's a nice snappy reply. Maybe you'll have another opportunity to use it.

LEO. Oh, I don't lack for opportunity. Even after all these years, it knocks with regularity. I'm constantly being offered forums for public confession. Really, it's very touching to know how many people are concerned about my moral rehabilitation. So eager to help me get this awful weight off my shoulders. This one woman — from some French film journal — for some reason I agreed to be interviewed for an article she was writing on my films. Turned out to be structuralist bullshit. Anyway, in the middle of it — here we go again. To be fair, we'd had a bottle of wine and we were getting along. Anyway, I informed her as affably as possible that I really didn't want to get into that subject. And she leaned forward and took my arm with that easy familiarity that a shared bottle of wine can encourage, she took my arm and looked into my eyes and said, "But Leo ..." Not "Monsieur Greshen" but "Leo," right? "But Leo," she said, "you will feel — how do you say it? — the relief, no?"

BENNY. And you don't think you'd feel relief?

LEO. Benny, please. To step into a mess of dog shit once — that's something that can happen to anybody. To intentionally step into the same dog shit again —

BENNY. What dog shit is that?

LEO. Look, I've been through this before. "Leo, get up, get it off your chest. You'll feel better, swear to God." All I had to do was submit to a nice dirty ritual of public cleansing. Did you read the Navasky book?
BENNY. I glanced at it.
LEO. Well, I think a lot of it is double-talk. But he got that part right. The ritual part. Get up in front of the Committee, admit your errors. Prove how repentant you are — *demonstrate* your sincerity by naming a few names, you'll emerge redeemed, rehabilitated. Decent American folks will be happy to shake you by the hand, slap your back, let you do your work. Now, though, different political truths are operative, as the saying goes. Now I'm told that I bought the moral equivalent of a pig in a poke. I got myself the wrong brand of cleansing and rehabilitation. There's a new improved formula. Yes, there is! This season, if I want to be cleaner than clean, I'm supposed to get up and say I done wrong when I said I done wrong before. I'm supposed to do a *mea culpa* over my other *mea culpa.* Only instead of doing it in front of a mob of congressional Neanderthals, I'm supposed to confess to someone like Navasky or that French structuralist or that kid at Avery College. And after I choke out my apology, Navasky, on behalf of his enlightened readers, will dispense absolution. "Go and sin no more." In my book, it's the same damn ritual of public cleansing, only some labels have been changed to conform to the spirit of blacklist chic. Well, like I say, I stepped into that shit once. I'm not doing it again. Not even for you, Benny. And believe me, you're about the only reason I'd think of doing it.
BENNY. Sounds like you've got this all thought out.
LEO. It's not like I haven't had the time.
BENNY. Just one problem, Leo. When you called me up that night, you didn't call me because you thought you were right. You called me because you felt lousy about what you were going to do.
LEO. Benny, I never claimed to feel good about it.
BENNY. But you did it.
LEO. Only a fool fights the drop.
BENNY. You want to translate?

LEO. You've seen enough cowboy movies. If the bad guys have got the drop on you, it's crazy to draw on them. You're only going to get gunned down. Can't fight if you're dead.
BENNY. So now we're cowboys?
LEO. Thank you for taking what I have to say seriously.
BENNY. Seriously, OK: Leo, not only did you not fight the drop, you helped the bad guys gun down some good guys. What would the kids in the balcony say if Roy Rogers shot Gabby Hayes?
LEO. Bad guys, good guys —
BENNY. It's your analogy.
LEO. I said nothing about good guys.
BENNY. Oh, I see: there were no good guys?
LEO. Present company excepted, of course.
BENNY. No good guys. Well, that makes it nice and convenient, doesn't it? If everybody's equally scummy, then the highest virtue is survival. That must make you pretty goddamn virtuous. You should write a book about your philosophy, Leo. Really. I've got the title for you: *Charles Darwin Goes to the Theatre.*
LEO. Being a victim doesn't automatically entitle you to a white hat, Benny. It's that old liberal impulse — romanticize the persecuted.
BENNY. What the hell would you know about liberal impulses?
LEO. Hey, I've got my share of them.
BENNY. You — a liberal? Don't make me laugh.
LEO. I sure wouldn't want to do that, Benny — make you laugh.
BENNY. Maybe you're a checkbook liberal. You send in contributions to those ads with pictures of kids starving in South America, a couple bucks to the ACLU —
LEO. More than a couple of bucks, but never mind —
BENNY. More than a couple? Well, hey, that changes my opinion completely.
LEO. I'll tell you where I part company with a lot of them, though. I won't romanticize. Just because someone's a martyr doesn't make him wise and good and pure. Sure, I sent in

money to Joan Little's defense fund, but that doesn't mean I'd trust her to baby-sit my grandchildren.
BENNY. The guys the Committee went after weren't accused of murder, just of having believed in something unpopular. And the ones who wouldn't buckle under — out with the garbage.
LEO. Which is exactly what they did to each other when they were members of the Party. Those bastards were always brow-beating each other, excommunicating each other for not embracing "the correct revolutionary line." Do you remember when the Party endorsed Henry Wallace for President? Lenny Steinkempf got up in a meeting, said he thought it was a crappy idea. So what did the Party do? They threw him the fuck out. And after *they* threw him out, his *wife* Elaine, being a loyal Party member, *she* threw him out. As far as I was concerned, facing the Committee was an exercise in déjà vu. Believe me, Nixon and Mundt could have taken lessons from some of those old Commies. I wasn't about to put my dick on the block for any of those guys. Why should I keep faith with them when they couldn't keep faith with themselves?
BENNY. The point wasn't to keep faith with *them.* Leo, don't you remember anything about how or why we put together the New Labor Players?
LEO. Oh, for Christ's sake!
BENNY. For Christ's sake what?
LEO. *(Laughing.)* Benny, you aren't seriously going to hit me with the New Labor Players?
BENNY. And why not?
LEO. All that agitprop bullshit, the slogans, screaming our lungs raw —
BENNY. Worthless?
LEO. Not worthless, exactly —
BENNY. Then *what,* exactly?
LEO. All we ever did was play to people who felt exactly like we did. Invigorating — sure. Fun — absolutely. And a great way to meet girls. But don't try to tell me we ever accomplished any great social good. I doubt that we ever changed anybody's mind about anything.

BENNY. That's how you measure it?
LEO. You measure it differently?
BENNY. Seems to me there's some value in letting people know — because they laughed or maybe cheered at the same time as a bunch of other people — letting them know they aren't alone. That there are other people who feel like they do.
LEO. Maybe we should have broken out some red pom-poms while we were at it.
BENNY. Pom-poms?
LEO. Hey, if you're going to cheerlead, you should have pom-poms. "Give me a P, give me an R, give me an O, give me an L!"
BENNY. Leo —
LEO. *(Continuing.)* "Whattaya got? Proletariat! Whattaya got? Class struggle! Whattaya go? Dialectical materialism! Rah, rah, rah!"
BENNY. Some terrific joke, Leo. Very funny.
LEO. What's funny is you telling me this stuff.
BENNY. What's funny about that?
LEO. You think I don't know my own spiel when I hear it?
BENNY. Your spiel?
LEO. Of course my spiel. "Class consciousness is the first step. Through theatre we give dramatic form to our lives and hopes and so create our identity and the identity of our community." You like it? I've got another three or four hours of this. Rousing stuff, hunh? *(A beat.)*
BENNY. Yeah, I thought so.
LEO. Oh, I convinced myself pretty good, too. But I'm not a twenty-two-year-old kid any more, and neither are you. And I'm not going to let you get away with pretending that *Capitalist Heaven* and rest of it was any great golden age of drama. Face it, Benny, it was amateur night.
BENNY. I'm not talking about how sophisticated or how professional. Leo, what I'm saying is that when we started, all right, we may not have had much polish or technical expertise, but we did have a sense of purpose. There was a *reason* I started acting. There was a *reason* Mort Kessler started writing. There was a *reason* you started directing. And then came a point you gave

up your reason so you could keep on directing.
LEO. Maybe directing *was* my reason.
BENNY. What — directing anything?
LEO. Of course not.
BENNY. You say of course not, but I don't take it for granted that there are things you wouldn't direct. Before the Committee — yes. But after?
LEO. So all of a sudden I'm a whore. Of course, it isn't whoring to do some dumb-ass sit-com. What was it called — *Rich and Happy*?
BENNY. *Rich But Happy.*
LEO. I stand corrected. Truly edifying, uplifting stuff. My God, in the old days, if somebody had told you that's what you'd end up doing! *Rich But Happy.* I mean, back then just the *title* would have made you gag!
BENNY. I had to live.
LEO. So did I, Benny. So did I.
BENNY. But if I did crap — and God knows I'm not holding up *Rich But Happy* as an example of high culture — but if I did crap, I didn't destroy other people to do it.
LEO. I don't happen to think that the work I did after that *was* crap. As a matter of a fact, a lot of it was damn good.
BENNY. If you do say so yourself.
LEO. You're going to tell me that it wasn't? Oh, I know this riff. If a guy's politics aren't approved, aren't correct, then he can't be any good as an artist. I bet you're one of those people who think God took away Frank Sinatra's voice as a punishment for voting Republican.
BENNY. I'm not talking party affiliation —
LEO. I know what you're talking about: In order to be an artist, you've got to be a certified good guy.
BENNY. Being a *mensch* enters into it, yes.
LEO. And if he isn't, you feel cheated. Shortchanged. Well, if art by bastards upsets you so much, you should drop everything right now, go into your library and toss out anything you have by Robert Frost. Now there was a world-class shit! And how about Ezra Pound! And let's not bring up Wagner!
BENNY. I don't have any Wagner in my house.

LEO. No? Well now *there's* a brave stand! My hat's off to you, Benny! Keep those doors guarded. Be vigilant! Hey, you can't be *too* careful. I mean, you never know when somebody might try to sneak the fucking *Ring Cycle* into your house without your knowing it, right?

BENNY. This I'm enjoying — you linking arms with Wagner!

LEO. Tell me something, if you found out that Charles Dickens *shtupped* ten-year-old boys, would that make him any less of a writer?

BENNY. Well, it sure as hell would make a difference in how I read *Oliver Twist.*

LEO. Whatever you or anybody else thinks about me as a person, I did good work, Benny. Not just before. After, too.

BENNY. I wouldn't know about after. I didn't see most of it.

LEO. Well, you missed some good stuff. If you don't want to take my word for it, you can take it from the critics. You can look on my fucking mantle in New York at the prizes and the plaques —

BENNY. I'm sure they would blind me.

LEO. They mean something, Benny, even if it's fashionable to sneer at them. They mean that a lot of people thought that the work was good.

BENNY. And that's important to you.

LEO. Yes, it is.

BENNY. You like having the good opinion of others.

LEO. Is that a crime?

BENNY. No, I don't think it's a crime. I like it, too. I'm just sorry to have to tell you that you haven't got my good opinion, Leo.

LEO. And I'm sorry to have to tell you I don't give a damn.

BENNY. Then why are you here?

LEO. Because I don't want your goddamn daughter walking out of my goddamn play.

BENNY. Fine, you told her that. So why are you still here?

LEO. Because I'm a masochistic idiot!

BENNY. What, you expected me to throw my arms open?

LEO. No.

BENNY. Then what?

LEO. Damn it, Benny — thirty years! It's been more than thirty years! We're going to start *dying* soon! *(A beat.)* While there's still a chance. *(A beat.)*
BENNY. Leo, you got a car?
LEO. Yeah. Why?
BENNY. Let's say for the sake of argument there's someplace you want to go. So you go to your car, put the key in the ignition — nothing. It isn't working. But there's this place you want to go. You want to go there real bad. You take a look in my garage, what do you know? — I've got a car. A car in good working condition. It's got a few years on it, but it runs fine. We're talking about a respected make. So you ask me, can you take my car? I say no, I'm sorry, I've made plans, I need it. You tell me about this place you want to go, how important it is to you to get there. I say I'm sorry, but no, I can't let you have my car. What do you do? You take it anyway. Now what do you figure I do in a situation like this? Call the cops, of course. Give them your description and the license number, they take off after you. What happens if they catch you? You end up being charged with grand theft auto. All right, you didn't steal my car. But there *was* someplace you wanted to go, and the only vehicle you could get your hands on was something else that belonged to me. *(Norma has entered during the above. Neither Benny nor Leo betrays any notice of her presence. Which is not to say that they don't know she's there.)* Something that belonged to me, something that belonged to Morty, something that belonged to a few other guys. I don't know how you did it with them, but I get the famous phone call. You call and tell me what you're going to do. You cry about the pressure. You tell me how much getting to this place you want to go means to you. You want me to tell you, "Sure, Leo, go ahead. Take it for a drive. Barter it for the good opinion of a bunch of cynical shits. Buy yourself a license to work." But it doesn't play that way. I say no. And the next day, you go into that committee room, and you use it anyway. The difference between that and you taking my car — my car you can return. *(A beat.)* Leo, I'm not Morty Kessler. I won't put it aside. I'm sorry. *(A beat.)* Norma, Mr. Greshen dropped by to ask you about his show. Why don't you tell him

what you've decided? *(A beat. Norma doesn't respond.)* Norma? *(A beat.)*

LEO. Miss Teitel, I would appreciate it if you would call me later. *(Norma nods. Leo exits. A beat.)*

NORMA. OK, I think I've got it now.

BENNY. What is that?

NORMA. Why you didn't throw him out before. All these years, you've been thinking, working up what you would say if you ever met him again —

BENNY. Who wanted to meet him again?

NORMA. I'm saying "if."

BENNY. I did my best to make sure that wouldn't happen.

NORMA. I'm sure you did.

BENNY. I gave up my favorite Chinese restaurant. A place I knew he sometimes ate. Never went back. Last thing I wanted was to see him.

NORMA. Last thing, hunh?

BENNY. If you'll have the stenographer read back the transcript, I think you'll see that's what I said.

NORMA. I know you said it —

BENNY. But you — with your years of wisdom and experience — you see the deeper truth, is that it?

NORMA. Maybe *at first* you didn't want to meet him again —

BENNY. Oh boy, here we go —

NORMA. Maybe in the beginning —

BENNY. I can see where all this is heading. I didn't, but really underneath it all, I did.

NORMA. After all, you had the speech ready. What good is a speech if you don't give it?

BENNY. And there it is, folks — my soul naked and quivering.

NORMA. Then why did you come out in the first place? If you knew who I was talking to —

BENNY. This isn't a Chinese restaurant. This is my patio. I won't stop coming here.

NORMA. That's not what I'm saying.

BENNY. Oh, you grant me the right to step out on it if and when I please?

NORMA. Sure, and it pleased you to do it then because he was out here.
BENNY. I should hide inside?
NORMA. Nobody said anything about hiding.
BENNY. What about Leo? It sure pleased *him* to barge in here uninvited.
NORMA. We're not talking about him.
BENNY. No? Oh, I see, *you're* setting the agenda here. The topics of discussion. Sorry, Mr. Chairman.
NORMA. Mr. Chairman?
BENNY. Mr. Silverman, you aren't being cooperative. If you would please answer the question. Did you or did you not know that the American Committee for Spanish Freedom was a Communist front organization?
NORMA. Pop —
BENNY. And just exactly who was present that night in Mr. Kessler's house?
NORMA. If you can't tell the difference between me and the Committee —
BENNY. The tone is similar, believe me.
NORMA. You're misunderstanding —
BENNY. I don't know what you think you're accusing me of —
NORMA. I'm not accusing you —
BENNY. No?
NORMA. I'm not disagreeing with anything you said to him.
BENNY. Then what? That I said it at all?
NORMA. Never mind.
BENNY. What — are you afraid I lost you your job?
NORMA. No.
BENNY. That's it, isn't it?
NORMA. The job isn't yours to lose.
BENNY. Right. Your decision.
NORMA. That's what he said.
BENNY. And you can take it from me, he's a man to be trusted. Yes, sir.
NORMA. I just hope you got what you wanted.
BENNY. And what might that be?

NORMA. I don't know. Satisfaction?
BENNY. No way to get satisfaction.
NORMA. Then why do it?
BENNY. Sometimes you do a thing because you've got the right to do it. Or don't you think I have the right?
NORMA. Of course you've got the right. And I've got the right to do some things, too.
BENNY. Like to judge me, my behavior? Well, I beg to differ, kiddo. You haven't earned it.
NORMA. Oh, so it's like with the painting. I don't have the proper background, so I can't appreciate it. Because I didn't suffer through the blacklist, I can't have an opinion.
BENNY. Have any opinion you want, but don't expect me to get all worked up about it.
NORMA. No, of course not. Who the hell am I, anyway? If I happen to think that walking around spitting battery acid at the world is no kind of a life —
BENNY. I don't have to listen to this.
NORMA. Pop, he did a shitty thing to you. No argument. But after all of these years, to let it keep eating at you, to let it take over your life —
BENNY. "A shitty thing." Your command of the language — "A shitty thing." Like maybe he stole a girl from me or got drunk and peed in my swimming pool. It goes beyond. You think something happens and that's it, it's over with? That it's gone and remote because you can stick a date to it and a lot of calendars have been tossed out in the meantime? All those books you've read, all that time in the library, you still don't understand a thing. *(A beat.)* I was an actor. Basic to being an actor is the fact that you can't do it by yourself. It's not like plumbing or fixing shoes or painting a picture. You've got to do it *with* other people in the *presence* of other people. If someone does something to cut you off from them, you're not an actor any more. I don't care what you call yourself or what you put on your resumé, you're not. You can't grow, you can't develop. You're not allowed to be what you could. You aren't even allowed to be who you are. You're an exile. Not just from your profession, your business. You're an exile from yourself. That's

what Leo did to me when he said my name. This charming fellow with all of his stories and his reasons. Sorry, yes. I'm sure he is. But that's what he did.

NORMA. And that's what you want me to do to myself. Because you couldn't work, you want me to refuse to work. Doesn't what you were saying apply to me as well? About needing other people to be an actor? You were entitled to work. Aren't I entitled, too? Or am I supposed to give up my entitlement because I'm your daughter?

BENNY. But with *him.*

NORMA. Since when do you have to like everybody you work with?

BENNY. Fine, you want the part, you keep the part. It's your decision.

NORMA. Pop —

BENNY. No, I think it's a terrific career move. And as far as your not liking him goes, I'll bet you get past that. I'll bet you two get along great. After all, so much in common: he steals my name, you throw it away.

NORMA. What do you want? You want me to blacklist myself?

BENNY. I want you to go ahead and do what you're going to do and spare me the hypocrisy of pretending that you give a good goddamn about what I want. *(Benny exits. A beat. Norma turns to the audience.)*

NORMA. That afternoon, I move to a motel. We go back into rehearsal a couple days later, a couple weeks later we open. True to his word, Pop doesn't come to the opening. The next day, I drive over to see him. *(Benny enters with brushes and paint, goes to the easel. He begins to work. A beat.)*

BENNY. The reviews?

NORMA. Mostly good.

BENNY. What about for you?

NORMA. Also good.

BENNY. Congratulations. *(Norma takes out a program.)*

NORMA. Something I want to show you.

BENNY. What is it?

NORMA. The program.

BENNY. What about it? *(Norma opens it to a specific page, hands it to him.)*

NORMA. Here.

BENNY. Your bio? I'm familiar with your credits.

NORMA. I added a line to the end. *(A beat. Benny looks at it, reads.)*

BENNY. "Norma Teitel is the daughter of actor Benny Silverman." *(He hands the program back to her.)* It's not enough. *(A beat. She stands there as he goes back to painting. The lights fade on them.)*

NOTES

Having participated in a number of productions and readings of this play, I thought I'd pass along a few of the things I've learned about it, as well as some background information actors and directors might find useful in building characters.

First, a technical matter. Norma's monologues to the audience should be kept as casual as possible. She simply has the ability in the middle of a scene to turn and address them. The lighting designer may be tempted to dim the lights and put a spot on her during the longer stretches. It's a temptation that should be resisted. Having seen a production in which this approach was tried, I can report that the audience interprets this an indication they're watching a memory play. But *Names* is not a memory play. I do not intend for the audience to think that Norma is recounting something that has happened to her, but rather that she has the ability to turn to the audience in the middle of ongoing action. To that end, I urge that normal lighting be maintained during such passages. While she talks, Benny should just keep doing whatever he's been doing and pay no particular attention to what she says.

In the beginning section between Benny and Norma, it's important to keep the tone light. If Benny blasts through the jokes, trying to go for laughs, not only won't it be funny, but the audience will have trouble buying the love they have to believe is between these two. For Benny, articulating the humorous or ironic side is as natural as breathing and requires little or no effort.

At this point, maybe I should tell you a few things I know about him. He's from a working-class Jewish background, the son of immigrants. He never had the opportunity to get much schooling, which is something he regrets, though he has made up for a lack of formal education by reading a lot, attending lectures and going to museums. As Leo says, Benny was working in the garment district when they were introduced. Leo gave Benny his first encouragement as an actor. Leo also was the one who introduced Benny to politics. In effect, Leo served as both an artistic and political mentor for Benny. Benny looked up to him, relished debating with him, loved working with him.

Neither Leo nor Benny was a serious member of the Party. They attended a few meetings, and they were in sympathy with a lot of the Party's avowed social aims — support for the civil rights movement, the enfranchisement of labor, socialized medicine, etc. But both left after a short time because they couldn't swallow the rigidity of the Party line. Still, even this short flirtation was enough to get them into trouble during the McCarthy era.

And when the McCarthy era came, Leo caved in under pressure, gave HUAC the names they demanded — including Benny's — and continued his successful career as a film and stage director. Benny, on the other hand, did not cooperate. He took the fifth. Not that Benny had any particular brief for the Party after he left it. Benny's refusal to name names was in defense not of the Party but the principle that people have the Constitutional right to believe whatever damn fool thing they want. He refused to cede to HUAC the authority to force him to publicly recant his old beliefs or to bring trouble to others by naming names. As a result of his stand, Benny was blacklisted. What he did was courageous, but being barred from his profession left a residue of bitterness which, thirty years later, still colors his dealings with the people around him.

Benny and Norma's mother divorced while Norma was still a child. Norma stayed with her mother in New York. Benny went to California in the late 1960s and, the blacklist no longer in force, became a regular on a hit sitcom which lasted seven or eight seasons and can still be seen in syndication. Every now and then he does a supporting role in film or a guest shot on a show, and he used to occasionally do a play for the hell of it, but he considers himself to be retired. And he's enjoying his retirement. He's reading, he's painting, he's listening to his huge collection of classical records, and sometimes he plays cards with a few old friends.

Because of the physical distance between them, Benny and Norma didn't see a lot of each other when she was growing up. Having had primarily a long-distance relationship, they usually talked on the phone about her immediate concerns — her schooling, her career, etc. Though in her teens she became aware of what her father went through, prior to the action of the play she had little opportunity to discuss the specifics with him. But here she is, staying in his house, and now they have the time to talk about these matters. What's more, she's now old enough to question some of his judgments and challenge some of his choices.

The first matter over which they square off is her name change. Yes, the change upsets him, but after some playful wrangling, he ultimately signals his acceptance of her decision. The second matter is the issue of her appearing topless onstage. Their difference on this topic illustrates the difference in their aesthetics. Again, he signals his acceptance of her decision. And then the main question between them arises: will she work with the man who named him to HUAC?

Benny asserts that the choice is hers, but there is little doubt as to how he wishes her to choose. The stakes are raised when Leo arrives at the house to force the issue.

The scene between Norma and Leo is perhaps the most difficult section of the play. Norma has to walk a fine balance between conflicting impulses. On the one hand, she's talking to a very powerful, gifted and impressive man. She hasn't decided yet whether to leave the show, and she's conscious that she may have to work with this guy, so she's not overtly hostile. Also, she has been caught off guard by his surprise appearance, so it takes her a bit of time to catch her breath and get her balance. On the other hand, she is indeed her father's daughter, and she refuses to be steamrolled by Leo. She wants to hear what he has to say for himself. In a sense, she's got him auditioning for her.

Leo is aware of the irony of his situation. (Like Benny, Leo breathes irony.) Yes, he's auditioning for her, but he's trying to create the illusion that it is up to her to please him. He keeps asking questions, challenging her assumptions, trying to gain advantage by putting her on the defensive, trying to disarm her wariness with humor. He is also trying to pretend that what she decides is not of great importance to him. This, of course, is not true. After all, he has taken the extraordinary step of coming to see her in dangerous territory.

What does Leo want? For one thing, as he says, he wants Norma to stay with the show. He is indeed tired of being walked out on because of something he did nearly thirty years ago. But he also wants Benny's friendship again.

A little bit about Leo's background. Like Benny, he is the product of an urban Jewish upbringing. Though he went to college and can quote Goethe, there is nothing dandified about him. He still has more than a little of the streets about him. It was largely through his vision and his passion that the New Labor Players was born. (He probably was in the habit of making the kind of inspirational speeches for which Harold Clurman was famous.) Whether or not they are handsome, people with passion are very attractive. They are great seducers. Benny was intellectually seduced by Leo, as were a lot of others. (Leo didn't only seduce intellectually. He saw that he was attractive to women and made the most of his sexual opportunities. In fact, there can be a bit of a sexual undertone to his early scene with Norma. I emphasize "a bit.")

It should go without saying that Leo feels some guilt for what he did to Benny. But, in my judgment, it would be a mistake to do anything overt to signal or indicate this guilt. In fact, an attitude which could be read as a *denial* of guilt will get the idea across more effectively. One should not lose sight of the fact that Leo is a very proud man and one who puts a certain amount of energy into putting a smokescreen over his vulnerabilities. To get back to the question of what Leo wants, he wants Benny to forgive, but he wants forgiveness without asking for it, though he comes damn close to doing so. When he finds himself alone with Benny, Leo's tactic is to try to recreate the old rhythms of their friendship — the banter, the jokes, the shared confidences. If he were to be explicit he would say, "You see, Benny? You see what fun it is being together again? Just say the word and we can do this all the time. Forget about the bad feeling and the politics. The truth of our relationship is the good time we have together, our shared history, our shared values."

And Benny is mightily tempted. He almost succumbs a couple of times. When Leo asks him what happened to the marriage, Benny is just about to confide in him as he used to, then he wakes up to Leo's game and pulls back. But Benny can't just throw Leo off his patio. He's going for something, too. If he can just get Leo to acknowledge that what he did was wrong and to apologize, then maybe.... But the apology implicit in some of what Leo says is not enough. He wants Leo to say the words.

He wants the words not just for moral vindication, but so that he can allow himself to be friends with Leo again. The scene between the two men works best when one can feel how much these guys have in common, how much, underneath the jockeying and the jabs, they still love each other. These two know each other in ways that nobody else does; to be cut off from each other is to be cut off from important pieces of themselves. This is part of the point I try to make humorously with Leo's articulating the same objection to nudity onstage that Benny had made to Norma before. As much as Benny would like to draw a clear line between himself and Leo, he keeps running up against the fact that the two of them have an enormous amount in common.

Ultimately, when Benny begins the car speech, it's not an act of rage; rather, it's informed by the deepest regret and sorrow. Though for years he's dreamed of the satisfaction he would get from telling off Leo, when the time comes he gets no pleasure, no thrill from it. Making the speech causes Benny as much pain as being on the receiving end causes Leo.

The scene between Benny and Norma immediately following Leo's exit is another hard one. Norma thinks she understands the truth, and by means of what she intends as Socratic questioning, she tries to get Benny to see what she has come to believe, that his refusal to let go of his bitterness is self-destructive. She genuinely hopes to help her father find some peace. But Benny is not about to accept moral instruction from his daughter. He tries to get her to appreciate his perspective ("I was an actor ..."), but when she refuses to quit the show, he turns on her angrily. In the last scene, when she makes a conciliatory gesture by showing him that she's included him in her bio, he replies "It's not enough."

At one point, I was discussing the script with a star who was interested in playing Benny. He told me that his doing the play was conditional on my changing the last line. He felt he couldn't play a character who would say such a thing to his own daughter. So he didn't play the part. I wrote the script so as to get to that last line. Part of the point of the piece is that suffering is not necessarily ennobling. Having been blacklisted, Benny is now blacklisting. He was denied his rights as an actor because he refused to make the gesture that HUAC demanded (to be a friendly witness), and now he is turning from his daughter because she has refused to make the gesture that he has demanded (to quit the show). The moral civil war that was the McCarthy era is echoed in the conflict between father and daughter. Dalton Trumbo once said that those days produced "only victims." Thirty years after the fact, new casualties are still being added to the list.

Incidentally, those with access to E-mail are welcome to post questions and comments to me at DGSweet@aol.com I will try to respond as time allows.

PROPERTY LIST

Canvas (BENNY)
Easel (BENNY)
Paints (BENNY)
Brushes (BENNY)
Playscript (BENNY)
Bowl of chips (BENNY)
2 beers (NORMA)
Theater program (NORMA)

NEW PLAYS

• **TAKING SIDES by Ronald Harwood.** Based on the true story of one of the world's greatest conductors whose wartime decision to remain in Germany brought him under the scrutiny of a U.S. Army determined to prove him a Nazi. *"A brave, wise and deeply moving play delineating the confrontation between culture, and power, between art and politics, between irresponsible freedom and responsible compromise." --London Sunday Times.* [4M, 3W] ISBN: 0-8222-1566-7

• **MISSING/KISSING by John Patrick Shanley.** Two biting short comedies, MISSING MARISA and KISSING CHRISTINE, by one of America's foremost dramatists and the Academy Award winning author of *Moonstruck*. *" ... Shanley has an unusual talent for situations ... and a sure gift for a kind of inner dialogue in which people talk their hearts as well as their minds...." --N.Y. Post.* MISSING MARISA [2M], KISSING CHRISTINE [1M, 2W] ISBN: 0-8222-1590-X

• **THE SISTERS ROSENSWEIG by Wendy Wasserstein, Pulitzer Prize-winning author of *The Heidi Chronicles*.** Winner of the 1993 Outer Critics Circle Award for Best Broadway Play. A captivating portrait of three disparate sisters reuniting after a lengthy separation on the eldest's 50th birthday. *"The laughter is all but continuous." --New Yorker. "Funny. Observant. A play with wit as well as acumen.... In dealing with social and cultural paradoxes, Ms. Wasserstein is, as always, the most astute of commentators." --N.Y. Times.* [4M, 4W] ISBN: 0-8222-1348-6

• **MASTER CLASS by Terrence McNally. Winner of the 1996 Tony Award for Best Play.** Only a year after winning the Tony Award for *Love! Valour! Compassion!*, Terrence McNally scores again with the most celebrated play of the year, an unforgettable portrait of Maria Callas, our century's greatest opera diva. *"One of the white-hot moments of contemporary theatre. A total triumph." --N.Y. Post. "Blazingly theatrical." -- USA Today.* [3M, 3W] ISBN: 0-8222-1521-7

• **DEALER'S CHOICE by Patrick Marber.** A weekly poker game pits a son addicted to gambling against his own father, who also has a problem but won't admit it. "*... make tracks to DEALER'S CHOICE, Patrick Marber's wonderfully masculine, razor-sharp dissection of poker-as-life.... It's a play that comes out swinging and never lets up -- a witty, wisecracking drama that relentlessly probes the tortured souls of its six very distinctive ... characters. CHOICE is a cutthroat pleasure that you won't want to miss." --Time Out (New York).* [6M] ISBN: 0-8222-1616-7

• **RIFF RAFF by Laurence Fishburne.** RIFF RAFF marks the playwriting debut of one of Hollywood's most exciting and versatile actors. *"Mr. Fishburne is surprisingly and effectively understated, with scalding bubbles of anxiety breaking through the surface of a numbed calm." --N.Y. Times. "Fishburne has a talent and a quality...[he] possesses one of the vital requirements of a playwright -- a good ear for the things people say and the way they say them." --N.Y. Post.* [3M] ISBN: 0-8222-1545-4